D1592885

THE WORLD OF OCEAN ANIMALS
DOLPHINS

by Mari Schuh

pogo

Ideas for Parents and Teachers

Pogo Books let children practice reading informational text while introducing them to nonfiction features such as headings, labels, sidebars, maps, and diagrams, as well as a table of contents, glossary, and index.

Carefully leveled text with a strong photo match offers early fluent readers the support they need to succeed.

Before Reading

- "Walk" through the book and point out the various nonfiction features. Ask the student what purpose each feature serves.
- Look at the glossary together. Read and discuss the words.

Read the Book

- Have the child read the book independently.
- Invite him or her to list questions that arise from reading.

After Reading

- Discuss the child's questions. Talk about how he or she might find answers to those questions.
- Prompt the child to think more. Ask: Have you ever seen a dolphin? If so, where was it? If you haven't seen a dolphin, would you like to?

Pogo Books are published by Jump!
5357 Penn Avenue South
Minneapolis, MN 55419
www.jumplibrary.com

Library of Congress Cataloging-in-Publication Data

Names: Schuh, Mari C., 1975- author.
Title: Dolphins / by Mari Schuh.
Description: Minneapolis: Jump!, Inc., [2022]
Series: The world of ocean animals
Includes index. | Audience: Ages 7-10
Identifiers: LCCN 2020050349 (print)
LCCN 2020050350 (ebook)
ISBN 9781636900513 (hardcover)
ISBN 9781636900520 (paperback)
ISBN 9781636900537 (ebook)
Subjects: LCSH: Dolphins—Juvenile literature.
Classification: LCC QL737.C432 S42873 2022 (print)
LCC QL737.C432 (ebook) | DDC 599.53—dc23
LC record available at https://lccn.loc.gov/2020050349
LC ebook record available at https://lccn.loc.gov/2020050350

Editor: Jenna Gleisner
Designer: Michelle Sonnek

Photo Credits: scheffan/Shutterstock, cover; Mark Subscenic Harris/Shutterstock, 1; Neirfy/Shutterstock, 3; Tory Kallman/Shutterstock, 4, 6-7tl, 6-7br, 12; Universal Images Group/SuperStock, 5; Binoy B Gogoi/Shutterstock, 6-7tr; COULANGES/Shutterstock, 6-7bl; Aqua Images/Shutterstock, 8-9; R. Maximiliane/Shutterstock, 10-11; Matt9122/Shutterstock, 13; Doug Perrine/Alamy, 14-15; Martin Prochazkacz/Shutterstock, 16, 17; Schnapps2012/Shutterstock, 18-19; vkilikov/Shutterstock, 20-21; Don Mammoser/Shutterstock, 23.

Printed in the United States of America at Corporate Graphics in North Mankato, Minnesota.

Dedication: For Sadie, Serafina, and Caruso

TABLE OF CONTENTS

CHAPTER 1

FAST AND PLAYFUL

A bottlenose dolphin leaps out of the ocean. It jumps high. Then it dives back into the water!

seaweed

Dolphins are playful. They chase one another. They even play with seaweed.

Risso's dolphin

Ganges river dolphin

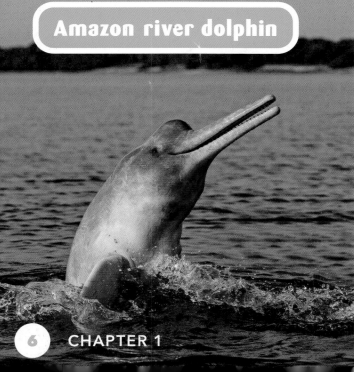

Amazon river dolphin

bottlenose dolphin

There are at least 40 known dolphin **species**. Risso's dolphins have round heads. Ganges river dolphins have long **snouts**. Some male Amazon river dolphins are pink! Bottlenose dolphins are gray. They are the most well-known species.

DID YOU KNOW?

Bottlenose dolphins can be up to 13 feet (4.0 meters) long. Orcas are the biggest kinds of dolphins. They can be more than 30 feet (9.1 m) long!

Bottlenose dolphins live in warm ocean water around the world. They sometimes swim in rivers. Some live in deep water. Others live near the **coast**.

TAKE A LOOK!

Where do bottlenose dolphins live? Take a look!

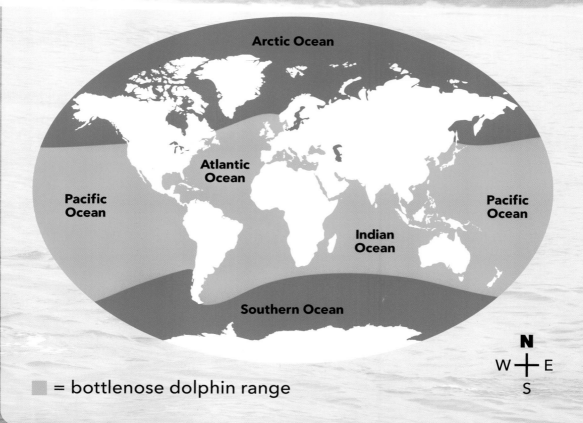

Arctic Ocean

Atlantic
Ocean

Pacific
Ocean

Pacific
Ocean

Indian
Ocean

Southern Ocean

N
W E
S

■ = bottlenose dolphin range

Dolphins are fast swimmers! They have rubbery gray skin. It is smooth. This helps them glide through the water. Flippers help them **steer**.

Dolphins hold their breath while they swim. They come to the surface for air. They breathe through their **blowholes**.

TAKE A LOOK!

What are a dolphin's body parts called? Take a look!

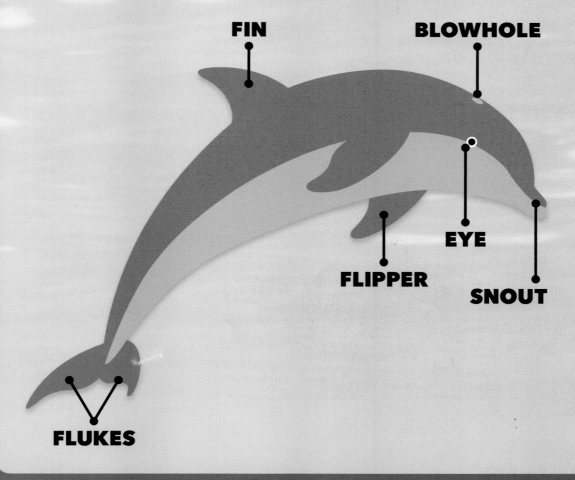

FIN

BLOWHOLE

EYE

FLIPPER

SNOUT

FLUKES

CHAPTER 2

PREDATOR AND PREY

Bottlenose dolphins often live in groups called **pods**. Some pods have only a few dolphins. Others have more than 1,000! Pods often change. Dolphins leave one pod to join another. They might do this many times a day!

Members of a pod stick together to stay safe. They work together to chase away **predators**. Sharks hunt bottlenose dolphins. **Blubber** also helps keep dolphins safe. This thick layer of fat protects them. A shark's teeth cannot always bite through it.

tiger shark

Bottlenose dolphins eat fish, squid, and shrimp. They work as a team when they hunt **prey**. They **herd** fish together into a ball. Then it's time to eat!

DID YOU KNOW?

Dolphins are smart. Some bottlenose dolphins put sea sponges on their snouts. Why? This protects them as they hunt on the rocky ocean floor.

CHAPTER 3

SURVIVING IN THE OCEAN

Dolphins whistle, squeak, and click. Why? These sounds send messages to members of their pods.

Click, click, click! The echoes from the clicking sounds help dolphins **sense** what is around them. This is called **echolocation**. It helps dolphins find prey. It also helps them find their way in dark water.

Each dolphin makes its own whistle sound soon after it is born. Dolphins know one another from their whistles. They can even remember other dolphins' whistles after being apart for 20 years!

Dolphins are **mammals**. Females give birth to one **calf** at a time. Just a few days after birth, a calf can make sounds. It stays with its mother for at least one year. The calf drinks its mother's milk. Its body makes blubber. The calf grows up and swims with the pod!

DID YOU KNOW?

Climate change, hunting, and **pollution** harm dolphins. Fishing nets harm them, too. Dolphins can get caught in them. How can you help keep dolphins safe?

calf

ACTIVITIES & TOOLS

ECHOLOCATION GAME

Play this fun game to see how echolocation works!

What You Need:
- a few friends or classmates
- blindfolds
- one adult

❶ **Pick one player to be the dolphin. Ask this player to sit in the center of the room. Ask him or her to put on a blindfold.**

❷ **The other players will act as fish. They will walk clockwise around the edge of the room. When the adult says to stop, all the fish will walk to the corner of the room that is closest to them.**

❸ **The dolphin player claps twice. This is like a dolphin making a sound. Then the fish players clap twice. This is like an echo that returns to the dolphin.**

❹ **The dolphin player listens carefully. He or she points to the corner of the room where most of the fish might be. Then all the fish players in that corner sit near the dolphin player.**

❺ **When the adult says "swim," the game continues. The last fish player becomes the next dolphin player.**

GLOSSARY

blowholes: Nostrils on the top of whale and dolphin heads that are used for breathing air.

blubber: A thick layer of fat under the skin of some ocean animals.

calf: A young dolphin.

climate change: Changes in Earth's weather and climate over time.

coast: The land next to an ocean or sea.

echolocation: The practice of finding objects by using sounds and echoes.

herd: To move animals together in a group.

mammals: Warm-blooded animals that give birth to live young, which drink milk from their mothers.

pods: Groups of dolphins.

pollution: Harmful materials that damage or contaminate the air, water, or soil.

predators: Animals that hunt other animals for food.

prey: Animals that are hunted by other animals for food.

sense: To feel or become aware of something.

snouts: The long front parts of animals' heads.

species: One of the groups into which similar animals and plants are divided.

steer: To make something move in a particular direction.

INDEX

TO LEARN MORE

Finding more information is as easy as 1, 2, 3.

❶ Go to www.factsurfer.com

❷ Enter "dolphins" into the search box.

❸ Choose your book to see a list of websites.

FACT SURFER